THE CATERPILLAR & THE BUTTERFLY

NATIONAL LIBRARY OF AUSTRALIA

A catalogue record for this book is available from the National Library of Australia

Published 2022

ISBN: 978-0-6454300-6-6 (epub)
ISBN: 978-0-6454300-7-3 (paperback)
ISBN: 978-0-6454300-8-0 (PDF)

9 780645 430073

Published with the aid of Jumble Books and Publishers (jumblebooksandpublishers.com)

The Caterpillar & the Butterfly

Autobiographical Poems

by

Richard Greene

For my granddaughter Bayla Rose, her legacy.

Bayla Rose, age 7, summer of 2021

Winter's Child

On this solstice day
in my 82nd year
my first grandchild was born.
The sun stood still for her.
(December 21, 2013)

Contents

The Boy Within

Noticing the photo on my bookcase
of a boy being kissed by a dog.
I think to myself
that boy is me,
65 years ago,
and I think
somewhere in me
that boy still exists.
Yes, I no longer look the same.
My hair is gray.
my skin no longer smooth.
I wear spectacles.
I have a beard!
Yet, looking at that boy,
I feel we are one,
as if the boy were like a butterfly
lurking within
a caterpillar's skin.

What's in a Name

I've never cared much for my name.
It's always seemed prissy to me
suggestive of well-scrubbed little boys
in brown velvet rompers with Eton collars
or short pants and glasses,
or middle-aged men whose trousers are always
neatly pressed.

The name echoes too of my mother's sharp
    "Richard!"
when I'd misbehaved
or wasn't paying attention,
and its subtly pejorative ring
in the mouths of other boys,
real boys not being called by their proper
    names,
not Henry or James but Hank or Jim.

Lord knows
there've been enough macho Richards,
the Lionhearted for obvious example,
or Wagner.
But somehow the name has become
associated with propriety.
Who was the model?
Was there any?
What sort of fate did parents suppose
they were spinning for their offspring
when they gave them this name?

In recent years I've taken to using Richard
as a distancing device,

a formal appellation
like the name on a business card.

I don't like Dick much better.
Though it may have been suave in the twenties,
and, aside from its other connotations,
it was what my father was called,
for I suffered the additional indignity
of being a junior,
and my father was one
with whom I didn't identify.

His was an easy case.
His parents, old-world Jews,
wanted a new-world name.
What could be more remote from the shtetl
than Richard?

As for Rick
that seemed to me like a name affected
by denizens of the society column,
the sort who play polo
with playboys named Raoul or Lance.

Maybe Dickie was the attraction for my mother,
a little boy one could willingly embrace.
My wife calls me Dickie,
as did my mother in good times.

Hard Passages

It was hard coming into this world
squeezed amidst moans and cries
through a too narrow passage
from a warm and comfortable place
into a cold, exposed and unfamiliar one
then suddenly seized by the feet
swung into the air
like an animal caught in a snare
and slapped hard on the back
by a hand half my size.
Could the end be any harder
than the beginning?

Early Me

Looking at a photo of myself
toddling across a lawn
arms upraised for balance,
I find it hard to envision
being so small,
looking out of so low a place,
standing hardly higher
than my mother's knee.

No, I have no recollection
of such a me.

A Birthday

There's a difference of opinion in the family
as to whether I was three or four.
I remember a coconut cake in the shape of a
   lamb
surrounded by yellow cotton chicks.
I see it as through a scratched lens.

Frozen Fields

My grandmother drove me to the train
that winter I was four,
through the threadbare fields of Indiana
with their ragged patches of snow.
I was on my way
to my mother in New York,
excited about the journey
and the prospect of being with her again,
but I remember
not so much the excitement
as passing through those wintry fields,
as if time were deep-frozen
in memory.

West Side Memories

We lived across from the planetarium,
mere yards from the sky,
while just down the street
was the el,
and still vivid
under the long-gone girders,
a barbershop
with its candy-striped pole
and carousel pony
astride which young clients sat,
at the center of the universe.

First Grade

I was in first grade when I was five
and my memories of it are so nebulous
I can't be sure
whether they're memories
or dreams.
I picture low, rambling buildings
of vague design,
the excitement of a track meet
in which older boys enviably competed,
and making parachutes
of handkerchief, rock and string,
hurling them as high as we could
and watching them drift down slowly
drift slowly down
through a dim haze
of memory
or dream.

Truckin' on Down

In the thirties,
when I was six,
we lived on Riverside Drive
and across from our apartment,
in the park,
was a small stadium,
with a big red apple
over its entrance arch.
Dance contests were held there,
bringing a bit of Harlem to midtown.
I watched from the window of our apartment
and though I remember little
of that place in which we lived,
the dancers are still visible in my mind
performing that rhythmic,
finger-shakin',
high-steppin',
bouncy walk,
truckin' on down,
in memory.

Under the Apple Boughs

There was a wall along the road
where we played soldier
behind the loosely stacked stones.
Next to it a row of mountain birch
tops tinted in memory with evening sun.
Then the house
in dappled coat of whitewashed brick,
and the orchard with gnarled trees
where we pressed apples on chill fall days
and savored the cold, sweet cider.

Outside my bedroom window
a camellia tree glistened,
and, beyond, a broad lawn
sloped down to the pond
where frogs held nightly congress
and I learned of mallards
and snapping turtles
and green-winged teals.
There we skated in winter
until darkness hid the agate surface,
and swam impatiently in spring,
the ice barely melted,
as if our innocence protected us from cold.

Between pond and house
stood a lone apple tree
where, as I watched at first light,
pheasants gathered
in their courtly plumage
to feast on windfalls.

Then bombs fell on Pearl Harbor
and soldier games gave way to war.

A Boy and His Dog

I still remember,
though it was almost seventy years ago,
the day my parents brought her home.
I was seven.
When I came home from school, they said
"We have something for you"
and ushered me into the pantry.
There was a puppy
with its crushed velvet fur,
not yet collie silk.
Love at first sight.
Her tail wagged.
My heart beat faster.
I named her Duchess
thinking it aristocratic, I suppose.
In my teens I thought it corny
but now I see it fit her long collie nose.
That was close to three quarters of a century
    ago
but I still remember what she looked like in
    that little room.

The Pond

There was a pond in my young years,
a place of reeds
reflected trees
and silky brown water
spilling over a weed-bearded dam,
a place where we swam from early spring
and skated in the early darkness of winter
    evenings,
a place of mysterious depths
where creatures vanished
into a green void
while tadpoles and minnows
swarmed on its verges
like exclamation points.

There I saw mallards, come down softly,
cruise, smoothly as pedal boats,
their broad feet massaging the water
until, sighting edibles,
they flipped forward,
to my delight,
as if on hinges.

There sometimes I surprised a frog,
hypnotized by my nearness,
stared into its knobby eyes
and saw its throat throb nervously.

There turtles sunned themselves
still as stones
while I waited, equally unmoving,
determined not to be the first to stir.

It was a small pond
but a world in my eyes.

Snapshot

I have a photo of me with my mother
from over sixty years ago.
I'm eight years old
wearing shorts and long socks,
standing close by her side
her arm around my shoulder.

We're next to our house,
the house we left a few years later
when my father went to war,
a house that ornaments my memory,
with its whitewashed brick,
its dormer windows,
one of which opened into my room,
its large sloping lawn,
the pond at the bottom of the hill
and the orchard on one side.

I visited that place a few years ago.
It wasn't the same.
The young trees in the photo's background
were large or gone.
The loose fieldstone wall
had been replaced by a high, mortared one.
The house next door and its acres of lawn
(with the collie that ran free
stalking pheasants in the dawn)
had been transformed into a development.
Even its topography had changed.

On the other side,
where "the knoll"

and our meadow once stood
was now a church,
hidden by a grove of trees
but not the apple trees of my childhood.

And on our once outer edge of town
the open fields had disappeared
diced into little lawns.
And my mother has been gone now
for almost fifty years.

Dog Photo

I am eight.
Duchess is kissing me
with blissful spontaneity,
her long collie muzzle
thrusting up lovingly
into my face.
I am smiling
with a mixture of appreciation
and the reflexive reaction
of one being tickled
by a very wet, canine kiss.

Radio Times

There was the opera
my parents tuned in to every Sunday,
in the background like a movie score,
but of little interest to me,
but then The Inner Sanctum
with its creaking door
and shivery stories
that sent me fleeing
down the long hall
to my parents' bedroom,
and The Shadow,
who knew what evil
lurked in the hearts of men,
and that other crime fighter
of mythical proportions
The Green Hornet,
whose theme song was
The Flight of the Bumblebee,
which strikes me now
as biologically incorrect,
and The Lone Ranger
whose theme was
an Italian overture
commemorating
a legendary 14th century
Swiss patriot,
and Jack Armstrong, The All-American Boy,
which posed the existential question,
"Have you tried Wheaties,
the best breakfast food in the land?"

The Other Side of the Woods

There was a woods
near where we lived
when I was eight
that I often explored
without ever reaching the other side
forever distracted
by a clear brook
and its teeming tadpole populations,
green flashes of leaping frog,
elusive salamanders,
bird-crowded bowers,
furry creatures
glimpsed hurrying through the undergrowth,
large outcroppings of rock
(castles of the imagination),
raspberries ripening in late summer.

I fancied myself one of those woodsmen
I read about in my books
who ranged the vast forest
that once stretched
from the Atlantic to the Mississippi.
Years later
when I rounded the woods in a car
I found it was less than a mile across.

The Cider Man

My mother and stepfather had a couple
working for them
in White Plains
between my seventh and tenth years.
Ida and Edward.
I remember their names
though that time in my life seems scarcely real
    to me,
almost something I imagined or dreamed.
They were called the maid and butler,
the latter much to the mirth
of my father's family in the Midwest
where I spent my summers
and was clueless enough
to mention it.

Ida cooked,
and served me snacks in the kitchen after
    school,
while Edward was a factotum, as they used to
    say
even farther back than those pre-war days.
He set up a cider press
in the old orchard,
our first year there,
something like a half barrel,
made with staves.
I helped him,
mostly watched really,
press the cider
while my hands grew cold
in the chill fall air.

I can almost taste the juice
cool and still frothy from the press,
truer to the fruit than anything
you can buy in a store.

Then there were my ducks,
the three, from a much larger brood,
raised in the basement
where they survived, first, drowning—
Baby ducks can't swim. I didn't know—
then a rat.
They grew to large and robust birds,
those survivors,
but come December '41
I needed money for a Christmas present
for a girl I fancied at school.
I consulted with Edward
and he said he could sell the ducks.
I agreed without a qualm, as I recall,
the makings of a good capitalist.

But the war came along and sent me in other
      directions.
I never saw Ida and Edward again
and never thought to try
though in a way they were just as much a part
      of my family
as those whose blood ran in my veins.

Passover

I was eight
when I learned the four questions
(Why is this night different from all other
    nights?),
a duty reserved for the youngest child,
memorizing them in Hebrew
in the car
on our way from the suburbs
to my aunt's apartment in the city.

For me that night was a time
of waiting hungrily for dinner
through a drone of words
in a language I didn't understand,
a blur of readings, songs and prayers,
and of falling asleep after dinner,
drowsy from the ritual wine,
on a big bed covered with fur coats
that smelled of perfume.

I didn't get any thrill out of stealing the
    afikomen
while the adults pretended not to see,
and the questions I mouthed
weren't the ones I would have asked
    for it seemed unfair to me
that the Lord had hardened Pharaoh's heart
then punished the Egyptians for it.

It only occurred to me years later
that this holiday celebrated freedom.

World's Fair

"You may not be interested in war, but war is
interested in you."—Leon Trotsky

I went to my first world's fair
when I was eight.
As is the way with such events
it was more about us
than the world,
and refracted the future
through optimist eyes.
You wouldn't have known
from anything on display
that a cancer festered
in Europe's bosom
or that the most brutal of wars
was mere months away.
Nor was there any inkling
of the baleful new words
soon to be unleashed
on our vocabulary,
blitzkrieg, storm trooper, quisling,
kamikaze, Hiroshima,
Holocaust,
while the Futurama
with its ebullient guides
depicted a morrow
of shining towers
where poverty was ostracized.
Oh, the world looked good
in our neighborhood
in the spring of '39.

The Swing

I walked to school past Freddie's swing
and it sang its siren song to me.

"Come, Freddie's friend,
sit down and swing,
forward and back
forward and back.
Make my arc reach high
until your feet scrape the sky.
Soar and plunge
soar and plunge
until you feel your insides race
to keep pace
with the rest of you.
Feel the air thicken
claw at your clothes
press on your face.
Hear it rush by your ears.
Then hang your head back and watch
the clouds reel by
the clouds reel by."

And before I knew it
I was late for school again.

The Competitor

When I was a boy and played baseball
I always hoped
the ball wouldn't be hit my way.
I couldn't catch it
and didn't want to be under it
when it came down.
When I threw a football
the awkward spheroid wobbled
through its brief trajectory
without the slightest hint of a spiral
and when I picked up a bat
it seemed that it and the ball
repelled each other.
   I was always last to be chosen for a team
and that was just as well with me—
nothing expected
nothing lost—
except that I cared
like any man-child.
So I learned to use books.
They were heavy and hard
and full of words
that hurt more than stones or sticks.

The Harbor, 1939

It was before the glass towers.
The crowd of skyscrapers
in lower Manhattan,
sheathed in brick and stone,
looked so massive
someone arriving from Europe
might have wondered
how the island could bear the weight.

From my father's office,
high in one of those buildings,
you could see the ships,
some themselves as big as skyscrapers,
steaming across the harbor,
maneuvering into the big piers.
Best of all, the passenger liners,
in those pre-aviation days,
with their cargos of exotic passengers
or passengers going to exotic places,
as were, in my child's mind,
all those beyond this city
and the suburb where we lived.
Liners my father could recognize,
whose names he could supply,
the Queen Mary, the Normandie,
largest liners of their time,
names a boy could conjure with.

That was over 75 years ago.
but the image of those big ships,
gliding across the harbor,

smoke streaming behind,
still lingers in my mind.

September 1, 1939

Where was I?
At home in our tranquil suburb?
In school, or was it too soon?
Playing with friends?
Reading in my room?
Still at the lake perhaps
or on a train
coming home.
I don't know what time of day it was,
don't think I even heard the news.
My parents surely knew
but they must have said
best not tell the children.
Nor did I know of Kristallnacht
Munich
the Sudetenland
Anschluss.

It was probably summery still,
the leaves unchanged,
a calm September day.

A Boy's War

I was seven
when it began,
Anschluss, then Munich—
Kristallnacht slipped by
wholly unnoticed by me—
and within a year
blitzkrieg was loosed on Europe.

Then Dunkirk and the fall of France.
I heard the news on the radio,
but it didn't seem so momentous.
It was part of life as I knew it,
along with boyhood fantasies
like the warplanes I drew
and learned to recognize
daydreaming of playing the hero one day
by spotting an enemy.

If it hadn't been for my parents' hushed tones
even Pearl Harbor might have seemed
like some extravagant sports event,
for in my boyish mind
death was unreal,
and war a game.

Growing Up

While I was growing up in a comfortable
    suburb
a million and a half children
Jews like myself
died in camps,
not like the ones where I passed my summers.
While I dallied down the tree-lined street to
    school
past big houses and spacious yards
those other children
were turned out of their schools and homes.
While I studied Hebrew and piano
    lackadaisically
those other children learned firsthand
the meaning of the Kaddish and the dirge.
While I pushed away the food
my grandmother urged on me
those other children grew thin
till they seemed not much more than
    skeletons.
And while I lay in my familiar bed
in my lovingly furnished room
fretting, perhaps, about a catch I'd flubbed,
but nonetheless falling asleep easily,
those other children slept fitfully
disturbed by barrack sounds
and nightmares of men in jackboots
and the smoke from chimneys.

Mashed Potatoes

When I was ten
I graduated from my one room school
with less than a dozen students
to a larger one
a couple of miles from home
on a busy avenue
instead of a few hundred yards
down our quiet road,
with hundreds of kids,
most unknown to me,
and bigger,
many by as much as a foot.

But they had a cafeteria there
where they served mashed potatoes every day
for five cents a scoop
(this was 1941)
a creamy volcanic islet on your plate
with thick brown gravy
in its crater.
I've never tasted anything better.

Betty Greer

The first girl I admired was Betty Greer.
That was in sixth grade.
Girls I'd known before
though subtly alien
seemed not all that different from boys.
It was only in fifth grade
that they became creatures apart.
I went to a bigger school
where the kids weren't all from the
    neighborhood,
weren't almost family,
and something inside me changed.
Girls became yearned-for-from-afar beings,
like angels.
I sold my three pet ducks
or rather asked our handyman to sell them for
    me
(probably for somebody's dinner—
I didn't ask)
to buy angora mittens for Betty Greer
for the Christmas of '41
not realizing
that the world and its wars
had fated me to move on.

Riverworld

Where the small midwestern river
issued from its lake
running smooth and brown
under a translucent vault of willows
I went exploring
when I was ten or so
imagining myself a voyageur
descending the mighty Mississippi.

There I encountered exotic fauna,
catfish with their mandarin whiskers,
looking learned and wise,
mud-puppies emerging from the water
like the first sea creatures
venturing onto land.

There sandy banks
sank into sepia waters
and a sunlit world
was steeped in mystery.

Comic Book Hero

It's hard to believe
that I once read comic books,
me with my three university degrees.
I must have dreamt it.
Or maybe it was another life
before I got my karma straightened out.

Batman, Superman, Captain Marvel,
they couldn't have been role models for <u>me</u>.

Book Worlds

I'm nine or ten
seated at my rolltop desk
next to a dormer window.
It's a rainy day
and a pearl-gray glare
of cloud-scattered light
streams through the window
where the only landscape I see
is that of the book before me:
the ubiquitous forests
where Arthur and his knights
pursue their solemn quests;
or Sherwood
where Robin Hood and his men
display their courage and cunning;
the plain before Troy
where long-ago armies clash
and Hector and Achilles pass
on their way to immortality;
or scenes from Odysseus' adventures
where Cyclops and Circe and Sirens
lie in wait.

Such are the pictures that scroll by
on the gray screen of those days.

First Books

My mother and father gave me
a gold-embossed set of children's books
for my eighth birthday,
Treasure Island,
Gulliver's Travels,
Greek myths I read over and over,
Norse myths,
a book of poetry,
from which I remember best
Burns' *To a Field Mouse*
its Scots dialect engraved in my memory
like a language learned in childhood.

Then there was a book I'd asked my father for,
one I'd seen advertised,
The Book of Marvels,
sci-fi about Mars,
but my father mistakenly got instead
Richard Halliburton's *Complete Book of*
    Marvels,
with its pictures of
the Hanging Gardens of Babylon
the Colossus of Rhodes,
the Great Wall of China
Mount Everest,
the Taj Mahal
and more.
I leafed through that book again and again
until its pages were worn,
its places on Earth
so much more interesting than Mars.

There's a faded photo of me
from that time
holding, with both hands, a book
propped up on a child-sized, roll-top desk,
soft light streaming through a window.
Books were my friends in those days—
unathletic, a new boy in town, I had few
    others—
and so they have remained.

A World That Was

As I turn on the radio
this Saturday afternoon
opera swells out
from where I left the dial
and I'm transmitted back
more than half the century
to those peaceful prewar days
when I had no intimation
of what the future held,
and our radio
with its gothic wooden case
was tuned to the Met
in our living room.

I associated opera in those days
with dull times
when I was housebound
and would restlessly quarter
that thicket of sound
chafing for something to do.
For years after
I never cared much for opera,
but it sings to me now
of a world that was,
in a child's hopeful eyes.

Summertime

As a child I spent my summers
with a crew of cousins
at my grandfather's house
on a lake in Michigan
where we passed much of our time swimming
and trooping into town for ice cream, or
    movies.
Horror films were a favorite,
Igor pouring molten metal on us,
in three dimensions,
from the tower of Dr. Frankenstein's house
(which for many years made Victorian houses
synonymous in my mind with horror),
The Incredible Shrinking Man
fleeing a house cat bigger than a rhinoceros,
rubber dinosaurs
rampaging through *The Lost World*.
The youngest of the gang
I took all this seriously
peering out from between my fingers
through much of the show,
clamping them shut when the going got too
    scary.

Then there was the amusement park
only 12 miles away
(which at the time seemed far to me
as if distance stretched
in inverse proportion to one's size),
the fun house
with its whimsical mirrors
and the forced laughter

reverberating from its loudspeakers,
the papier-mâché monsters in the house of
    horrors
exciting more hilarity than terror,
and a large flat cylinder of a ride
that rotated so fast
you could hang on its inner side
defying gravity,
a sensation that visited me in my dreams.

The cousins with whom I spent those summers
over half a century ago
are still young in my mind
splashing into the lake,
filing into the little theaters
in Coloma and Watervliet
or heading out rowdily for that amusement
    park.

Pullman Memories

Riding a train
takes me back
to those boyhood summers
when I traveled alone
from New York to Chicago
starting from Grand Central Station
with a gentle jolt,
gathering momentum
past the vacant eyed apartments
of upper Manhattan,
wondering about the people
who lived inside,
then over to the river
where we hit full stride,
our wheels clicking
at a Dixieland pace,
the Hudson Valley scrolling by,
lake-wide river, stubs of old mountain,
the play of light in a cloud-crowded sky,
until we turned off at Albany
into mile on mile of farms and woods,
imagining myself into the houses
along the right of way,
those who might live within
seeming not quite real,
as we no doubt to them,
two worlds
sliding by one another
each in its own continuum
of time and space.

Then in the dining car,
self-conscious but proud,
the center of attention
in that adult place,
and not long after
in my berth,
snug as a tent,
shaken down to sleep
by the jiggling of the train,
waking during the night
when we stopped
at some anonymous station,
pulling the window shade up a crack
to see if I could make out a sign
of where we were,
watching the moving figures
swathed in steam,
silhouetted against the platform lights.

Then it was morning
and the flat fields of Indiana
were wheeling by,
telephone poles
riffling by
at a dizzy pace.
Like a horse
galloping back to its stable,
we seemed to accelerate
as we drew near our destination.
I felt I had to hurry getting dressed
lest I would still be in my pajamas
when we reached Dearborn Station
where the train might be shunted off

before I emerged,
my father on the platform muttering,
"Where is that boy?"
But we slowed down
as we swam into the denser urban landscape
and instead of being caught unprepared
I waited impatiently
for that endless city
to end.

The Lake

There was a lake in Michigan
where I spent my childhood summers,
a glacial lake
with hilly banks
scooped out of flat farmland.
A mile wide and three long,
it was big enough
for the far shore to seem a foreign place,
adding to the mystery of the water
with its large carp that hovered in the shallows
   like blimps
and its murky depths,
tall seaweed reaching up at you
as you swam into the deep water
where there were primitive slashing carnivores
alligator gar
rumored to have once attacked a man.

But there were also the sunfish and bluegills,
their rainbow hues visible in the shallows,
bass, streamlined and speckled,
minnows that would swarm away from you
flashing out of the water in formation,
and boats,
sailboats with their canvas wings,
small motorboats
their back-mounted motors buzzing
like insects of legendary decibels,
and the big ones with their inboard engines,
the Cadillacs of that watery place
emerging from their houses with a self-satisfied
   rumble

to turn and breast the water,
cleaving it,
filling the air with spray,
rocking smaller boats with their waves.

Then there was the Honeymoon
a two-decker
miniature version of the larger craft
that plied the far vaster waters of Lake
    Michigan.
It made the rounds of the lake on weekends
tooting its train-like whistle
and announcing over a loudspeaker
"Around the lake and down the river to
    Watervliet
on the Honeymoon."
Every weekend the Honeymoon,
regular as church bells.
The boat has no doubt long since been
    scrapped
but it still makes the rounds of the lake in my
    memory,
its ghostly speaker calling us in its wake.

Aficionados

When we were ten or eleven
my cousin Dicky and I
used to hike a mile
to the little store
down by the crossroads
to buy a cigar,
for our father, we said.
Then we'd slip the gold paper ring
it came with
   onto a finger,
and stroll back home
along a road
where nobody knew us,
puffing ostentatiously
and enjoying the shocked looks
of those we passed
in a trail of pungent fumes.

Fishing

There's a time at the end of the day
when the air grows perfectly still
and lake water smooth as syrup.
When I was a boy, I used to fish at that hour
hurrying through dinner
to row out on the silky water
ruffled only by the wake of my boat
and the rings within rings made by its oars.
Most evenings I'd cast my lure
dozens, scores, maybe hundreds of times,
the calm broken only by the whir of my reel,
the gurgling of the lure,
the occasional splash of a fish
leaping out of the water,
or a dog barking
somewhere on the shore,

but every once in a while
a bass would strike.

This Dove Is Not for Mourning

The mourning dove doesn't sound mournful to
   me,
wistful maybe,
but not melancholy,
as if happy with the day
whether a chill March one like this
or a sultry one in August.
For me it sings of childhood summers,
spent at the lake
where my grandfather had a house,
of warm mornings
when fresh from bed
I could comfortably step outside shirtless,
of times when I could hear
the trees' full rustle
and waves lapping the shore,
and see fish dimple the mirror of evening
and swallows swoop
over the languid water
streaked with gold.

Scent from the Past

Opening the back door this evening
I'm caught up in a scent of earth and vegetation
from over 50 years ago,
the dark aroma of the dirt road
I sometimes walked at night
along the lake where I spent my childhood
    summers,
the oil-calm water on one side,
a small tremor disturbing its reflections,
on the other side, interiors
stage-lit behind their window panes.

For a moment I think I'm seeing the lights
from houses next to that long-unvisited road,
but then I'm back in the present,
though the scent of that old ground
still tugs at my memory.

Watermelon Days

Here I am, a graybeard, eating watermelon
and remembering those summers
when I could count my age in single digits,
summers at the lake where my grandfather had
    a house
and all the cousins would assemble for dinner
around my grandmother's large table.
Though there's plenty of melon in the fridge
I find myself cutting close to the rind,
as I did in those days,
and there I am,
still that boy at seventy-three,
at the table with the tiffany lamp overhead
or descending the hill to the lake,
its remembered water, smooth and green,
lapping softly on the shore,
and the sound of mourning doves in
    counterpoint.

Seeing Water

Even now, in my sixty-eighth year,
I still experience a thrill
when rounding a curve
or topping a hill
I come upon a body of water,
whether festive blue
or sullen gray,
open to view
or half hidden by trees.
Even a small lake
I pass almost every day
still surprises me
with a pulse of pleasure.
It summons up, I suppose,
the lake where I spent
my childhood summers,
its mile-wide waters
abloom with sails,
where I fished
as day segued into night
and gold streaked
the sky's book of hours,

the remote Canadian lakes
where I basked in a solitude
broken only by the lonely cry of loons,
moose grazing in the shallows
or the occasional band of Cree
in their quiet canoes,
gathering wild rice,
and overhead at night
the sky-spanning, pulsating

polychrome curtain
of the aurora,

or the Hudson
where I whiled away my time
watching ships slide languorously by,
the slow kaleidoscope
of clouds and sky
over the Jersey bank,
or seagulls
gliding against the towering Palisades
so steady on their wings
the world seemed to move
while they stood still,
and in the background always
the tremendous harp of the bridge
gracing the river's canyon
as it might the very gates of heaven.

Then there's the Pacific
which, more precocious than Balboa,
I first saw at age six,
having come from the east
with my grandmother
who, indulging me,
drove straight to the water,
not even stopping
at our new home.
It was overcast that day
and I was disappointed
that the great ocean
wasn't the least bit blue.
Still, it was the Pacific,

spreading all the way
from California to Cathay
with a leap
only the imagination could equal.

Settling Accounts

When I was in seventh grade
we moved to Southern California
and my father
thinking, rightly, that I lacked machismo
thought to toughen me up
by having me wear short pants.
I was the only boy in my class who wore them
and attracted bullies
the way lawns attract dandelions.
There was one who lived on our block,
Richard Parker.
I used to cross the street to avoid him.

That was sixty-six years ago.
Today Richard Parker would be seventy-eight,
if still alive,
and I wonder what his life was like.
Did he drop out of high school
get a blue-collar job
become a ne'er-do-well
and turn to drink,
or go to college
and become an executive
known for ruthless workforce reductions,
or a Cheneyesque Republican operative?

I'd like to meet him again today,
when I'm much more robust
than most men my age,
and give him a bloody nose
and two black eyes.

Early Explorer

Living in L.A.
when it was much smaller than today
I ranged far
on my balloon-tire Schwinn
from our suburban fastness
eastward down the daylong boulevard
rolling the city's length,
like LaSalle
exploring the great mid-continental waterway,
past movie houses
and department stores
full of siren temptations,
past buildings monotonous as waves
toward the city's towered center
which I saw each time longingly from afar
but reached only once
having to turn back time and again
to be home before dark,

westward toward the ocean,
that shore I never reached,
picturing its blue expanse
with dogged anticipation
as I toiled my way
past mile on mile
of urban Gobi,

or over the high hills to the north
through untamed canyons
with their boulder strewn streams
and groves of scrub oak
to the range's far shoulders

overlooking a broad valley
that reached into the blue-gray distance
(imagining myself a pioneer surmounting
the last westward fold of the Sierra)
then down to the citrus groves
where I lingered
among multitudes of orange globes
in the welcoming shade.

The Girls of Summer

The lodge where we stayed last night
had iron in its water
like our house at the lake
where I spent my childhood summers
and as I was falling asleep,
one thing leading to another,
I thought of the Hutchinson girls
with their blond hair and bouncy curls.
seeing them in my mind's eye
on the lawn
between their big house and the breakwater.
The youngest was in her early teens
and I a couple of years younger.
They were my American dream.

They're probably grandmothers now,
if still among the living.

Freshman Goddess

There was a girl I admired
in my freshman year in high school.
Her name was Jill,
a name I've found piquant ever since.
I sat right behind her in one of my classes.
Was it Latin or algebra?
The subject is lost forever
in the vision of her honey blond hair
inches in front of me, all semester.
It was straight and glossy and cut in a pageboy
and I imagined I could smell its clean fragrance.
But I, still shorter than many of the girls,
though sitting so near,
was fated to admire her from afar.

Chickens in Beverly Hills

We kept chickens in Beverly Hills,
not in the early days
before it had become
an island of affluence
but almost half way into the 20th century.
It was during the war,
poultry and eggs were scarce
and my mother was not one
to worry about being déclassé.
So every day
after I pedaled home from Beverly High
I gathered eggs
in that henhouse
amidst the stars.

My First Nude

I remember the first nude photo
that came into my possession.
I was thirteen
a freshman in high school.
The photo
on a postcard mounting
looked like it was taken
before the first World War,
the subject Rubenesque
reclining on a couch
under heavy draperies,
painting-like, in a word,
except that she had a luxuriant bush at the
    crotch,
while mine was still sparse,
a fact that made her
all the more desirable.

The photo, which resided in my dresser
under the socks
disappeared one day.
My grandmother had confiscated it.
She didn't say anything, but I knew
because she scowled at me for a week
every time we passed on the stairs.

Woods

When in early spring
I pass a woods where the trees are budding
I feel like I'm back in those woods near military
    school
to which I escaped on weekends
with a fellow cadet, Duncan Tremaine,
wholesome as the sound of his name,
one of my few friends in that place
to which boys were sent
for discipline,
a place of the violent, uncouth and
    authoritarian—
those who liked to impose their will on others,
or who liked to live under the arbitrary order
of military life,
and those who fought it,
not out of principle
but because they liked to fight
or resisted all authority—
a place of southern chauvinism,
the civil war refought verbally
in the dorms at night
with the few boys from the north.

The woods were dimpled
with shallow hollows—
like cupped hands—
fringed with feathery budding leaves,
a different planet from the campus,
and I feel when I pass such places now
the freedom of those budding woods
and of being 15.

Too Long

It was military school
and we had to recite a poem from memory.
Most of the boys chose short ones
no matter the subject.
"If" was a favorite, as I recall.
I, however, chose another Kipling
"Gunga Din"
to demonstrate my machismo.
I remember many of the lines to this day
sixty-five years later.
"You may talk o' gin an' beer
When you're quartered safe out 'ere
And sent to penny-fights an' Aldershot it
But if it comes to slaughter
You will do your work on water
An' you'll lick the bloomin' boots of 'im that's
    got it"
I recited
with 14-year-old bravado.
But I fear I gave myself away.
No red-blooded American boy
would memorize a poem of 188 lines.

Through the Camera's Eye

When I was sixteen
I walked with my camera
into parts of the city
I'd only passed by before,
the Bowery
with its rundown hotels and bars
and the sad men
who frequented them,
a park where old immigrants
played bocci
behind a chain link fence
in front of tenements
festooned with fire escapes
and laundry lines,
down to the island's end
where you could see the rivers
on both sides
and subway lines
came out of the ground
laid bare like an anatomical display.
All this was new and strange
seen through the camera's eye.

Seventeen

That summer I worked at a camp
not far from the city
on the other side of the river.
One of the counselors, Didi—
Shirly Lutz, from Akron Ohio—
was a lithe, compact girl
with a sweet smell of sunlight about her,
and as she sat in the high lifeguard chair,
her smooth legs crossed,
the guys would crowd around
like stage door Johnnies
vying for attention.

Didi and I had the same night off
and we'd go into the city
down to the Village
and all-night smoky jazz,
heading back to camp
not long before dawn
taking the nearly empty subway
to the bridge.
The buses didn't run at that hour
so we'd walk the mile across,
solitary voices
high above the water,
the sun rising at our backs,
our shadows stretching out
long as the life before us.

Pictures Then and Now

Time was, unknown to most of today's youth,
before the spread of suburbia and the
    multiplex,
when we went to the movies in palaces,
not like Versailles or Buckingham, to be sure,
but rather vast dark chambers
where shifting light beams played on mote-
    filled air,
like sunlight falling through clouds,
where we passed our Saturday afternoons and
    evenings,
immersed in adolescent murmurings,
entranced by motley patterns on a screen
or necking in a place called the balcony
like courtiers in some ornate nook
surprised there by Watteau.

Six Feet

I remember aspiring anxiously,
to being six feet tall,
the height of "fine" young men.
"He's six feet now." I heard my elders say of
    others
masters of many accomplishments
to hear their parents tell it
but above all—above all—over six feet.
That was the measure of a man
in those quaint days
(as the days of one's youth are always quaint)
when the world was at its good war
and boys were going off
from Main Street,
and Park Avenue,
some to remain abroad forever
"six feet underground,"
as if that were deep enough
for a body to stand up
without breaching the surface,
and I, too young to go,
still strove to measure up,
5-7, 5-8, 5-9 and so on
until, hallelujah, six
then, glory be, an inch to spare,
an inch and more I've since lost
to the attrition of time.
But the pride still is mine
of having been taller than average.

High School

High school wasn't a high for me.
I was one of those
to whom it brought home
the ruthless stratification
to which this primate is prone.
No longer safe in the unjudgmental bosom of
    my family,
no longer sheltered by a mother's
    reassurances,
in the grip of pubescent hierarchies
as harsh as those of chimpanzees,
I began to judge myself
and was one of those who found themselves
    wanting.

The Taste of Summer

I remember picking blueberries
with my mother and sister and brother
on a sunny, breezy hill
overlooking our house,
the sky bright blue,
few clouds.
My mother gone over five decades now,
I can still taste those berries,
even this winter day
as I breakfast on blueberries,
brought from another continent,
and I remember my mother,
her auburn hair, her grey eyes, her voice,
on that berry-laden hill.

My First Poem

The first poem I wrote that I remember
was about the ice that piled up
on the shore of Lake Michigan
behind our Chicago home.

I was 15.
I showed the poem to a schoolmate.
She said it was trite.
I had to look the word up,
and wrote no poems
for the next two years.

Listening to Fats Waller

I think
this was the music of my mother's youth.
She danced like a flapper, I suppose,
something it can be hard
to imagine one's mother doing,
but she showed me the Charleston
when I was in my teens.
We danced it the only way you can,
energetically,
mother and son,
between the sofa and the baby grand.

Self-Portrait with Cigarette

The summer I was eighteen
I took up smoking
thinking it would enhance my image.
It wasn't the tough guy I had in mind,
not Humphrey Bogart
but some Sartre-like philosopher
wreathed in smoke,
like an oracle,
wielding the white wand elegantly
between long, slender fingers,
drawing the fumes deep into himself
as if they were charged with visions.
When I wasn't in the Village
at some off-Broadway theater, art cinema or
    jazz club
I paced the streets of Manhattan
perfecting my technique
suppressing the callow tendency to cough
learning to exhale through my nose
even blow smoke rings,
ironically of course.

In the end I was an accomplished smoker
but no more Delphic than before.

Self-Portrait with Boots

In the photo
I'm wearing riding pants and boots,
hands on hips,
cigarette dangling Gallicly from my lips.
I didn't ride,
but I had the boots made in Mexico that
    summer
because I thought they looked debonair
and actually believed,
though I would have denied it if asked,
that clothes make the man.

Hanging Out at MOMA

I first visited an art museum
in my early teens
because it seemed the thing to do,
but I didn't understand
what people saw in those walls full of pictures.
Then I had a hip young teacher
who was into modern art,
still somewhat new in those days,
and her pheromones blended in my brain,
with the art she advocated.
I became a champion of cubism and abstract
    art,
arguing heatedly with my parents
and other philistines,
and took to visiting MOMA
consorting with those angular dames
the Demoiselles D'Avignon
or contemplating a painting
by one Pavel Tchelitchew
of children in a tree
that looked like a photograph
of systems vascular and lymphatic,
or a nebulous galaxy.
I tried to read the meaning in it
as in everything I saw,
and the less revealed the more I read.
This, I imagine, is how art critics are bred.

Waiting for Love

For years when I was in my teens
I didn't fall in love
and began to fear I wasn't capable of it.
Fifteen, sixteen, seventeen, eighteen,
love didn't come.
It wasn't even clear to me
what love was.
I'd ask myself
"Is this love?"
and was unsure.
But I found out soon enough,
about that
and other aches.

Depressed among Poets

I was depressed in my youth
but my depression was of a humdrum sort,
not dramatic,
more a deadening
than a torment,
a sense of nullity,
less fire than ice,
not that of a Poe or Baudelaire
much less a Lowell or a Plath,
and, having poetic aspirations, I thought,
How can one make poetry of that?

Becoming T. S. Eliot

When I was young and impressionable
I wanted to be T. S. Eliot.
No matter that I didn't understand much of his
    poetry.
I felt a man of letters was the most admirable
    thing to be.
As for the physical heroes of yore,
I knew that wasn't me,
and, having been "poet laureate" of my eighth
    grade class,
I aspired to emulate
that paragon of modernity.
The first step I took
was to get horn-rimmed glasses
though it was arguable whether I needed
    glasses yet.
An aunt of mine said to me
with amazing perspicacity
(though she never even went to college)
"You may think they make you look
    intellectual,
but you'll have to wear them the rest of your
    life."
I kept them anyway
and wear glasses still
but, as far as I can tell,
they've done nothing for my poetry.

Joan

She was a grade ahead
and helped me with my homework
so we could play after school
as a result of which
I lagged in my learning
of multiplication tables.

We explored the woods
behind her house,
a brook with newts
and boggy ground
favored by jack-in-the-pulpits
and skunk cabbage,
talking of childish things.
On cold fall days
we would build a fire
and bake potatoes in the ashes
hovering near to stay warm.
When their outsides were charcoal,
their insides still hard,
we pulled them out
split them steaming in the cold air
and, too eager to wait for them to cool,
ate them gingerly
with a little salt.
We never reached the end of the woods.
It seemed so far,
though when I returned years later
it was just a stroll.

We used to make ourselves laugh
until the laughter became real.

Good buddies, in short,
though I was a boy
and she a girl.

One day a gang of us
were teasing another girl
and Joan, hands on hips
faced us down
with a stinging rebuke.

Not long after I moved away
We didn't see each other again
until years later
when we were young adults,
but she wasn't good looking,
and I was shallow enough to care.

The Trouble with Rilke

We were nineteen.
She took me to her room
and without ceremony
undressed.
Afterwards we discussed poetry
and, when, wanting to impress her,
I mentioned Rilke
she said he was a sham.
I was horrified,
not at her opinion
but at my unawareness
of what grounds she might have
for scorning such an icon.
The thought of asking
and revealing my ignorance
didn't cross my mind.
I never called her again
and don't remember her name
but I've remembered all these decades
what she said about Rilke.

The Poet in the Underworld

Almost every day for three years
I walked four blocks
to 22nd and Broadway
where I boarded the subway,
on rainy days
in wet socks
and in winter
when cold wind sliced
through the granite canyons
making underground almost welcome
but also on the gentler days of spring and fall
reluctantly leaving behind
the world with its leafy trees.

From there I rode uptown
to the caverns beneath Times Square
filled with shadowy fleeting crowds,
and thence to a portal at 116th
through which I ascended
only there to be interred
in law school's deadening halls.

Life and Times

Reading May Swenson's "*Riding the A*"
I'm beamed back in memory
to that time in my early twenties
when I daily rode the subway
between 23rd and 116th and Broadway,
reading my texts or *The Times*,
tranquilized by the rocking of the train
and the click clack of wheels on track,
rolling timelessly
through station numbers mounting
as the years
or counted down in memory,
and now I find those years alive
like images on celluloid.

Bivouac Weather

It was cold this morning
with wind driven rain
and when I went out for the paper
my mind was swept back 56 years
to when I was a young draftee
in basic training.
We bivouacked for a week
in weather like this
sweating under ponchos all day
while the rain drummed its fingers
on our helmets,
sleeping two to a pup tent
in flimsy government issue sleeping bags,
awakened after a few hours by the cold.
Some nights it was cold enough to snow
but it was worse when it rained
for if you brushed the tent in your sleep
rain seeped through where you'd touched it
smearing your sleeping bag with water
dripping on your face and neck.
But this morning
as I padded back to the house with the paper
I felt like I was 23.

Citizen Soldier

I was a soldier once
in a faraway land
though not on death's hallowed ground.
It was during an undeclared peace
and I went to an office every day
where I battled armies of paper,
and by night toiled in other ways
in beer halls and brothels.

There were field exercises, to be sure,
and Saturday parades
where we practiced maneuvers
unseen in warfare
since the redcoats were ambushed by the
    minutemen,
and our company commander
polished his patent leather holster
lovingly as an apple,
while we waited to march by
sharply aligned
as if all of one mind
our bodies going one way
our minds another.

Time and Again

Catching a glimpse through an open window
this mid-June night
of a circle of lamplight on the street
and the soft silhouette of the maple tree
in our front yard
I'm suddenly a GI in Verdun
almost sixty years ago.
It's May.
Winter finally vanquished by spring,
the streetlight in front of the barracks
shines through full new leaves
fragrant in the fresh night air,
and I'm just twenty-two.

Blossom Time

I remember the Massif Central
about this time of year
almost fifty years ago
that high ground
spattered with new leaves
small orchards blossoming here and there
but mostly a sprinkling of green
fresh as the clear streams
with their thin sheets of ice.
Why that spring
out of nearly seventy?
Perhaps it was freedom,
for I was a young soldier then
on leave
driving from Heidelberg to Provence.
Perhaps it was the solitude
after the enforced society of military life,
alone and free
driving down a country road in France
the world just greening
the streams still braced with ice.

Driving to the Sun

From Paris
to the Costa del Sol
we drove
in my dilapidated convertible
in the springtime of our lives
down a long, straight Roman road
tunneling through pines
on into Spain
drifting through Madrid, Granada, Sevilla
then to Málaga
the top down
Colette and Serge
perched on the seat backs
waving to the earthbound
as we sailed through small towns
on our way to the sky.

Remembering Vientiane

Known among early European visitors
for their gentleness and insouciance,
they lingered in a backwater
of this turbulent century.

I lived in their capital
near the broad Mekong
on a dirt lane
bracketed by old wooden temples,
unpainted and weather-stained,
with their muffled bells
and slow traffic of orange-robed monks.

Only roosters
disturbed the peace
until tanks came
clogging the narrow streets,
grinding them under ridged treads,
spewing manic metal
onto roofs and shutters,
like the rhetoric
of clashing ideologies.

And bodies erupted
from the river's smooth surface.

Bangkok Farewell

It was kite festival time
when last we strolled the parade ground
under grand paper birds and dragonflies
swooping over the long red slopes
of the temple roofs,
over the gaudy towers
encrusted with fragments
of porcelain and mirrors,
over the goliath guardian statues
with their fierce faces,
over the food stalls
and exuberant crowds,
and I knew I would see no more
your wayward beauty.

My Age of Aquarius

I happened to look at a picture
that's been hanging in our house for years
but seldom engages my awareness.
The picture's a drawing by my friend Lenny
of his wife Esther
pregnant and sitting on a bed, sewing.
It's from some forty years ago.

We were in Ecuador,
I working for our government
and Lennie escaping
from the materialism of American life,
or maybe the draft.
In photos from that time
I'm wearing long sideburns
and granny glasses.

So Lennie and I were pals.
He introduced me to pot
(I wasn't very precocious that way)
and I remember a moonlit night
we grooved on a chain link fence.

Esther was pregnant with Yamara,
a Quechua Indian name.
They later had a boy named Sparrow
who'd be in his thirties now.
I've wondered from time to time
how he fared with that name.

I heard that Lennie and Esther divorced,
but that was after I last saw them,

over a generation
and four Republican presidents ago.

Dream Life

My sister asked today
how old you were
and I remembered Cape Hatteras.
How many years ago?
Forty-three?
Summer? Spring?
You were young and slim and lithe,
and libidinous
the way I'd grown up believing women weren't.
Oh, I knew better by then,
but part of me still believed
and I was surprised and grateful,
and you were young and slim and lithe and tall.
Seventeen years we were together
then divorced, the children in school still.
The children are in their thirties now
and you sixty-three.
It's as if our life together were a dream.

We Said It Was Forever

even though we should have known better,
and we even thought it might be.
The first years
we continued to discover
how like we were.
We formed a tight compartment
like a bathysphere
proof against the world
and we decided
to make a child.
We felt it kick
in your swollen belly.
We chose names
one for a boy
one for a girl.
A second child.
Then unity
began to leak
out of our little world.

Till What Do Us Part?

We did it the way you're supposed to.
We married under a chuppah.
I stomped on a glass.
We had a reception at the Plaza.
We were even registered at Tiffany's.
But none of that prevented our marriage
from breaking apart.

Oldies but Goldies

We moved not long ago
and today as I unpacked our CDs
(compact disks, not certificates of deposit,
though I'm of an age to have those too)
my eye lit on "The Best of The Doors"
and faster than I could snap my fingers
a door opened on the time
when I first heard that group.
It was in the late Liberty Music Shop
in midtown
around the corner from Saks and Saint Pat's
between the secular and the sacred as it were
where you could audition records,
meaning listen to,
33 rpm in those days.

A woman in the booth next to mine
was listening to The Doors' new album.
I could hear it through the partition.
"Hello, I love you. Won't you tell me your
       name."
"Baby won't you light my fire."
"People are strange when you're a stranger"
       they sang
to a faintly raga-like beat.
I asked her what the album was,
having been out of the country for two years,
bought it forthwith
and hurried home to play it for my wife,
my then wife, that is.

I liked rock from the beginning,
though already a career man by that time,
liked everything Middle America found
    offensive,
wore my hair long, as long as I could in the
    State Department,
had sideburns and granny glasses,
was against the war.

The Doors,
then cutting edge
are gray haired now,
if still alive,
and their era is another country for the young
as the Roarin' 20s were for my generation.
CDs are disappearing too.
But 33s are coming back.
Maybe the Hindus were right
about cycles of history.

Being an Uncle

I just signed a letter "Uncle Dick".
That's what my many cousins
used to call my father.
When we gathered
at my grandfather's lakeside house
for the summer
the air was crowded with calls of Uncle Dick.

Now I'm the only Uncle Dick in our family,
yet I feel like a pretender.
It's as if I weren't old enough to be anybody's
    uncle.
It seems like dressing up in one's parents'
    clothes.
On the other hand, it makes me feel old.

Keeping up with the Times

I go out for the paper
in the watery predawn light
eager for word
of the administration's latest blunder,
new exposures of corruption in business or
    government,
the latest evidence that we're losing this crazy
    war,
yet more frenzy from the religious right.
I settle down in my armchair
put up my feet
turn on my reading lamp
and plunge with pleasure
into my daily ration
of indignation-worthy news.

Silly Man

I was a serious boy
and most of my life
rarely indulged in silliness.
Oh, I was prone to the inadvertent kind,
causing me to avoid the deliberate sort all the
      more.
Then I married a woman who liked my jokes
and gradually I extended them
into a bit of clowning.
She laughed and I clowned some more
and again she laughed.
I was energized,
like a dog walking on its hind legs
egged on by applause,
and the more my audience of one applauded
the more I two-footed it,
progressing to splits and fast buck-and-wings.
Now I even clown in public sometimes,
and when I do, publicly or privately
I feel lighter for it.
At this rate, I'll end up floating away,
like a helium filled balloon.

The Mating Dance

We met at a gathering of do-gooders.
I was invited by mailing list accident,
which is not to say that I didn't belong to the
    tribe.
We came up the stairs to the front door at the
    same time.
I was wearing a tweed jacket
with no doubt a tasteful shirt and tie.
"Hi" I said in my deep baritone "I'm Dick
    Greene."
Wow you thought, you later confided.

During the meeting I disagreed
somewhat too bluntly
with something you said.
Who would have guessed that before long
we'd be living together
for the rest of our lives?

The Love that Stayed

Once in my life, love came and stayed
took up lodging and never departed
fed well and grew plump,
yes, satisfied.
No more drama.
No more ache.
No more thrilling acrobatics.
It sits at table quietly now
while sometimes we converse
sometimes sit silent.
We no longer even say
I'll love you forever.
Yet it seems we will.

Suburban Girls

I grew up in a suburb
and as a consequence
have a thing for suburban girls
or, rather, the women they grow into.
Not that I have anything against city or country
    girls.
Just that they don't have quite the same appeal
    for me.
There are gaps in their backstory
as far as I'm concerned.
Those who grew up in the suburbs, on the
    other hand,
represent womanhood more fully in my mind.

So I married one from Glencoe, Illinois,
and another from Ridgewood, NJ.
Scarsdale, Shaker Heights, Germantown or
    Bethesda
would have done just as well
but one marriage worked out, the other didn't
which goes to show
that in romance,
unlike real estate,
location isn't everything.

Too Genteel

I like those brazen women
I see or read about,
or whose works I read,
who talk of sex uninhibitedly,
unblushing and unabashed,
aren't shy about their bodies,
wear tight skirts, little red dresses
and five-inch heels,
ride on the backs of motorcycles,
but I've never met such a woman
and if I did
she probably wouldn't be
the least bit interested in me.

Morning at the Pool

I swim weekday mornings
when there are few people at the pool
mostly senior citizens like myself
or stay-at-home housewives
and those of their progeny
too young for summer camp.
This morning a toddler
enjoying his first summer on two legs
totters precipitously at the poolside
while in the water I glide
through a net of sunlight
refracted by the waves.

Reading Matter

I've always been partial to children's books
not just for my children
but for myself.
I confess
I'd rather read Lewis Carroll
or Tolkien
than Ulysses
or Camus,
and I found in the Brothers Grimm
a good respite
from the drudgery of the law.
Now in my retirement
Harry Potter has arrived
just in time.

Looking Back

In the mirror this morning
I noticed a cowlick
not normally there,
from where the pillow pressed my hair.
Time was when that cowlick
needed no help to stand
but did so on its own
with the vigor of youth,
and I thought of the stages I've been through
and then of myself when the cowlick was fresh
and I looked at best a few years ahead,
incapable of imagining a much later self
and uninterested in the earlier ones,
for in my young years I rarely knew
where I was going,
or even where I'd been,
until I was well along the way
and the knowledge was of no use.

Going on Seventy

Sixty-ninth birthday today,
a day like any other
except for taking down
the box of old photos
from the closet shelf
and opening the album
where my life is laid out
in random intervals:
a toddler in motion
bald and pudgy
arms upraised for balance;
seven, reading a book
or playing with my dog;
a ten-year-old
serious, with younger siblings;
the summer before high school,
thirteen looking twelve;
sixteen, hands in pockets,
severe but nonchalant;
nineteen, with cigarette.

Then flipping through the years
as if peering into one of those devices
that riffle photos rapidly
making figures appear to move,
I progress through work and leisure,
sites scattered across the globe,
as friends appear and fade from view,
family members debut as infants
and swell to adulthood,
beards sprout and are reabsorbed,
bodies thicken,

hair grows long and short again
then stiffens and pales
down to the iron gray of today,
and, between the photos
all the hopes and fears.

Birthday

Dawn rose this morning on a clear sky
bearing only a few cupcakes of cloud
but gilded by a billion candle light.
Today I'm seventy-five.

Seventy-Five

I woke up this morning
suddenly three quarters of a century old.
I can look back on three generations
six dogs
a dozen Presidents
almost as many cars
and an even larger number of wars.
Yet I don't feel any older than I did yesterday.

Weddings

I remember the weddings,
remember them all.

My cousin Sue and her high school sweetheart
on leave from the Air Corps
in '44
First time I got high.
I was thirteen.
It was champagne,
at the Beverly Hills Hotel.

Brother Jeffrey and his Italian-American bride
with her large clan
at a country club in Pacific Heights.
Tuxedos.
Live orchestra.
Adults dancing with children
into the wee hours.

Brother Michael and Alice
at her parents' home
on a hill overlooking Boise.
Guys with long hair and wire-rim glasses.
The sky still light at ten o'clock
on that far western edge of the time zone.
My daughter, four,
in her long white dress with strawberries
glowing in the twilight.

Brother David and Elaine
in their adobe in Santa Fe
Elaine and her sisters

dancing sinuously while lip syncing to
"You Make Me Feel Like a Natural Woman,"
and my son, about eleven, dancing up a storm.

Sister Deborah and Rob
in wine country
in an old Victorian hotel
their friend singing in a sweet tenor
"Makin' Whoopee."

I remember others.
Those were just a few.
Three of them ended in divorce.

Sue, Sue, Kalamazoo

I was talking to my cousin Sue last night
about the old days
when she was in her teens and I in my pre-.
We were among the summer cousins
who used to assemble
at my grandfather's house at the lake,
stocking shelves in the storehouse of memory.
Cousin Sue's in her 80s now
and I in my 70s
and when we talk
we rummage merrily through those memories.

Last night Sue was talking about
how they used to pick me up in Kalamazoo
when I came from the East on the New York
    Central.
I don't recall the town at all
though I'm sure I was there more than once.
I conflate it in memory with another K
the Kellogg company
which is in Battle Creek,
not far away,
where they made some cereal,
the advertising slogan said,
by shooting it out of guns.
(Somehow that made sense to me at the time
though why that would sell a cereal
is beyond me now.)

I've another magic memory
of a town nearby,
Holland Michigan,

where they grew apples the size of grapefruit
too large to get my young hands around.

And then there's Glenn Miller's *I've Got a Gal
    in Kalamazoo*
which we used to listen to
on 78 rpm
in the sunroom
along with Harry James' *Sweet Sue*
and, in my mind, cousin Sue
<u>is</u> that gal from Kalamazoo.

Things I Didn't Say

I don't usually brush my hair
but did today
to ease out some obstinate tangles
and, as I did, I remembered my stepfather
    brushing his,
and the brush without a handle he favored
(the first time I bought a brush
I bought the same kind)
and a concoction he used on his hair,
bay rum and castor oil,
names redolent of an earlier time,
like those of patent medicines.
I began to think of what it was like for him
becoming parent to a moony boy of six.
Did he ever ask himself "How am I going to
    deal with this?"
Then I remembered an argument we had
when I was in my twenties.
Unhappy with my work, I was thinking of
    joining the C.I.A.
He let me know, tactfully,
that there might be some problems
with spying as a vocation,
and I reacted impatiently.
I never told him he was right,
and I never thought to tell him
how good he'd been with me.

Seventy-Six Going on Seventy-Seven

I recently moved to another state
and am frequently asked my age
as I sign up for this or that.
Each time, though I only say "seventy-six",
I think, with a mental titter,
"seventy-six going on seventy-seven"
for it reminds me of those long-ago days
when I was eager to lay claim
to being almost one year older.
"Six going on seven"
I'd say with a modest smile.
Now I state my age matter-of-factly
and the smile is wry,
but still with a touch of pride.
Of course I don't hope for my listeners to
    respond
"My, what a big boy."
It's another sort of compliment I'm fishing for:
"You certainly don't look your age."

Inheritance

I'm not much like my father.
You can see a family resemblance,
but he was a businessman
and cared deeply about money,
while the only poem he cared for was "If".
I, in venerable tradition,
disdained his commerce,
but today I said something in a voice
that reminded me of his
and I wondered
if I'm more like him than I care to think.

Every Day Is a Bad Hair Day

I have contrary hair,
sullen, argumentative, obstreperous.
I have to waterboard it to subdue it.

Facing the Music

I wasn't much of a dancer in my youth,
used to stand on the side of the dance floor
chatting nervously with similarly challenged
    boys.

I didn't talk to the girls either.
Didn't know what to say to them
any more than I knew how to dance.
(The two have a deep connection, I imagine.)

But recently in my fourth quarter of a century
a woman not much younger than myself
told me she was a terrible dancer as a girl
and I imagined myself sitting beside her at a
    dance
those many decades ago
conversing amiably
each confessing with a laugh that we couldn't
    dance
and maybe getting together to learn.
If only youth were so wise.

Identity

175 pounds of tissue, bone and fluid,
a mobile mechanism,
a biological machine,
myself at the controls
looking out from inside my skull.
I walk, I work, I swim, I dance
cogitate, manipulate
defecate, fornicate
eat, laugh, cry
talk, write, sing
and think therefore, It's me.

Multiple Personalities

There is a multitude of mes,
one who limns landscapes with words
or remembers nostalgically,
but hammers on human foibles,
one who meticulously observes the behavior of
    birds
but uses those observations
to ridicule human ways,
one who can be romantic
but punctures balloons,
one who's ever so serious
but makes raucous jokes,
one who's elegant
one who's crude
one who's decorous
one who's lewd.
Consistency is not among my faults.

Charm

When I was young I admired charm.
It attracted me to certain girls
and the Irish.
Jews didn't have it much, I thought.
My wife's been telling me for years
that I do
but I ascribed that to the delusions of love.
Then the other night
as I held forth at a dinner party
I realized it was true.
Somehow I'd acquired the elusive trait,
bit by bit perhaps
each increment indiscernible.
Now that it's mine
I distrust it,
as if I'm engaged
in some sort of sly deception
of which even I am not aware.

Terms of Endearment

I left my wife a note this morning saying,
You're a doll
and the other day
I called her my old lady.
That set me to wondering
about the origins of such expressions.
I remember old lady being used
in those movies they used to make
about motorcycle gangs.
Could it be a tender tribute
to a promise of permanence
among the famously footloose?

My regular name for her is sugarplum,
something fragrant and delectable,
always in season
in this alcove of Eden.

Her favorite for me,
currently,
is pumpkin,
though I'm not very round
or at all orange.
Huggie bear is another favorite
easy to decipher.
Then there's stud muffin
Why muffin?

But my favorite is bubeleh,
a fragment of Yiddishkeit,
out of the mouth of my
Italian-Polish, Roman Catholic wife.

My Wife Reminds Me

to send my children Hanukkah cards,
to call relatives and friends
I haven't spoken to in too long,
to send birthday cards,
to take my medicine,
to keep my doctors' appointments
and so on.
It reminds me of what Yeats' wife said when
    asked
what it was like living with a genius.
"Oh," she said, "I don't notice."

Becoming Dickie Again

I saw my cousin Bob last week
for the first time in decades
His hair is white now
and he looks older than his father did
the last time I saw <u>him</u>,
but he called me Dickie
and it made me feel like the Dickie I was
those many years ago.

Alternative Universe

I am living in an alternative universe
not the one I should have been born into.
In this one I say and do foolish things.
In the right one I'd be more surefooted,
so to speak,
my arches wouldn't have fallen,
I wouldn't remember all my lapses so vividly,
I'd practice what I preach,
I wouldn't use so much salt
or have such a craving for sweets
or lose my temper
or procrastinate
or have trouble remembering names and dates.
No, this is not the me that was meant to be.

Confessional

I've never been addicted
to anything stronger than cigarettes.
I've never even tried anything stronger than
     pot.
I've never taken to alcohol
aside from a few binges when I was in college,
experimenting with getting smashed.
So I've never been in a twelve step program
or struggled to get back on the straight and
     narrow.

I've never been in a deep depression
not even one that came up to my chest.
I've never put my head in an oven
other than to clean it,
the oven, that is, not my head.
I've never even seen the inside of a sanitarium
other than in pictures,
in something about Lowell I think.

I was never mistreated as a child
or at least not enough to cause permanent
     damage.
I've never been poor
or had to live in roach infested digs.
I've never even seen an indoor rat
or met anyone who belonged to a gang.
I've never had a life-threatening illness
or been in a serious accident.
I've never suffered overwhelming grief.

In short, you might say, I'm not a survivor.
I doubt my memoirs would sell.

Country Cousin

I've lived a good part of my life in large cities
but for some years I've dwelt in smaller towns.
Last weekend I was in Manhattan
for a cousin's birthday
and as I flowed with the crowds,
like a bath toy in a surging stream,
breasting the human waves released
when red lights turn to green,
dizzied by the rushing rivers of traffic,
I felt challenged,
like a swimmer caught in a tide
that's flowing out to sea.

Dwellings

Every place I've lived
still dwells in my mind
like ghosts in an attic.
I think Chicago and see
the apartment by the lake,
ice piled on the shore
one cold winter,
or the place near the railroad tracks
where I slept in harder times
on a cot rolled out at night.
The house in White Plains
when it was still country:
the meadow, the orchard, the pond.
New York, Los Angeles, Boston, Beverly Hills
Washington, Quito, Bangkok,
to name just a few,
so many cities
so many dwellings,
more rooms than Versailles,
but it's the houses that haunt,
not are haunted.

Deconstructing Superman

Superman, Superman,
there was a time when I read of your deeds
    avidly
awaiting each 10¢ issue of your chronicles
    eagerly
like a celebrity fan addicted to checkout
    counter magazines,
but that was before I became an intellectual.
Likewise Captain Marvel, the big red cheese,
and Batman.

Now grown out of my childish ways
I deconstruct those "superheroes" learnedly,
but the Joker and the Penguin,
they're real,
both cousins whose names I won't reveal
and many another I've known in my time.

Cufflinks

I recently found cufflinks in my dresser drawer.
It's hard to believe I ever wore them,
not much less vain than gold neck chains,
but while we consider neck chains woppish,
WASPs wear cufflinks,
or at least used to.
Still they weren't my style.
I thought of myself as an intellectual,
looked on the countercultural 60s
as the high point of American civilization,
disdained my cufflink-wearer father's style.
Still I wore cufflinks.
I guess I have them in my blood.

Confessions of a Bourgeois Gentleman

My life, I confess,
Has been largely without drama.
Oh, I spent a few days in a war zone once,
though not in combat.
I've had my share of depression,
but always of a low-key sort,
like a bad cold,
and endured small childhood traumas,
though nothing worse than being bullied,
or being the last one picked
when the boys were choosing up sides for a
    game.
Then there was the banal ache of rejection by
    the opposite sex,
and there was loneliness,
again not out of the ordinary,
but enough to give me an unencumbered view
of the poetry all around us.

Not Much of an American

I've never cared much for baseball or beer,
sitcoms or Frank Sinatra.
I thought *Gone with the Wind* was dumb.
Likewise *Casablanca*.
Disneyland leaves me cold,
ditto Disney World
and most of the works of Walt.

I didn't like Ike,
or J. Edgar Hoover,
and Ronnie reminded me of the Wizard of Oz.
I didn't care for John Wayne either.

I don't get a kick out of waving Old Glory
and can't get hot about guys burning it.

I never got a charge out of Mustang cars
or watching NASCAR races.

I root for the underdog
not the Yankees or Dallas
or dream teams in the Olympics.

I don't believe in UFOs
or that Elvis lives
and I think school prayer should be allowed
only if it's not out loud.
As for being born again, no thanks.

Put that in your pipe, dude,
and smoke it.

My Mother Who Died Young

I have a photo of her in a silver frame.
She's wearing a broad brimmed hat,
pearl earrings and a dress with a scarf at the
    throat.
Her eyes are blue, or green, or gray.
You can't tell,
the photo being black and white.
That was when she honeymooned in Havana,
almost eighty years ago,
but I remember well her gray eyes,
like those of some lady of Camelot.

Delete from Address Book

Last year it was my best friend from college.
Yesterday it was my brother-in-law.

Approaching my eighty-fifth year
the pace of deletions quickens.

Father to the Man

I used to lope down stairs.
Now I plant one foot
cautiously after the other.
Sometimes I trip going up,
not stepping high enough.
My arms and legs grow thin.
My right eye no longer coordinates well with
    my left.
I used to spend a great deal of time
undressing in my mind
women I saw on the street.
Now I sometimes have to remind myself
of gender differences.
But when reminded
I still harbor fantasies much like those
I had when eighteen,
and my likes and dislikes
are still much the same.
If I were to meet myself as I was then
I'd laugh in amazement
at how much I share with that youth.

I Like a Woman with Wrinkles

being of wrinkly age myself.
It's as if we were fellow immigrants
in the country of the young,
the fresh faced
and so often self-absorbed,
with their new enthusiasms
which they fancy
set the standards for all time.
No, give me a woman who knows
how fashions come and go
who's earned her wrinkles
with toil and grief
with whom I can empathize,
and compare notes.

I See Myself Becoming Old

My closet is full of suits I don't wear anymore.
Nothing I need to wear them for.
There are days when I stay in my pajamas till
    noon.
I picture my heirs looking at my wardrobe one
    day
asking "Can you think of anyone who can use
    these
or should we give them to Goodwill?"
Or, "Would you like this tie as a remembrance
    of Dad?"
As I read the obits of the recently deceased,
which I took to doing a few years ago,
I compare their ages to mine.

Then there's the arthritis in my hands and feet.
My left foot aches when I walk
and I suffered a rupture in a time-worn tendon
    not long ago.
I have more trouble lifting things and getting
    around.
Don't jump over puddles anymore
for fear of the damage I might do coming
    down.
(No more kicking up heels for me.)

What will it be next,
the incipient cataracts?
My hearing isn't what it used to be.
I don't think I need a hearing aid yet,
though my daughter disagrees.

Or will it be something unforeseen
like that ill-fated tendon?

I see myself becoming old,
yet it's as if I were watching it happen to
    somebody else.

How I Know I'm Getting Old

When I was young
and the Andrews Sisters were popular
I couldn't imagine what people saw in them.
I didn't care for their songs
or three-part harmony.
But basically it was what they stood for in my
    mind.
Though I knew no Andrews Sisters fans
I could imagine what they were like:
people who lived in tacky subdivisions
and voted for Eisenhower,
women with perms
who waxed orgasmic
over refrigerators,
and said things like
"Ladies first" and
"That's what little girls are made of."

Now when I hear the Andrews sisters sing
"Bei Mir Bist Du Schein",
or "The Boogie Woogie Bugle Boy of Company
    B",
nostalgia creeps over me.

What's a Century?

The receptionist asks my date of birth.
"March 23, 1931", I say
and think how remote that must seem
to the young woman behind the desk
in this year of our lord 2006.
Somebody born a century earlier than me
would have arrived in the Jackson presidency,
the first not of a founding father or one's son,
before the coming of the radio, the car, the
    airplane,
    the great building of railroads,
the war that almost split our young nation in
    two.
At my age, that man born 100 years before me
would have found himself in a wondrously
    different world
from that into which he came,
the modern world for all its later change.
But here I stand before this young woman
a representative of an era three quarters of a
    century past
and she probably gives it no thought.
In her job, she meets septuagenarians every
    day.
Besides, the young are seldom interested
in their parents' or grandparents' times
until it's too late.

End of an Era

Anita O'Day died yesterday
When I heard it on public radio
I told my daughter
and she said
"Who's Anita O'Day?"
Is this what it means for an era to end?

Disconnect

It's hard for the young to imagine
they ever will be old
or that the old were young once too.
But it's also hard
for me to believe
that I was ever young.
Oh, I know I was,
have the memories to prove it.
Yet sometimes those memories
don't seem quite real,
as if it were all a dream.

It's Hard to Believe We Were Ever So Young

Looking through old photos.
Cousin Sue and I in Chicago
in front of one of those courtyard buildings
recognizably of the place and time.
I must have been four,
Sue eleven.
She's now eighty-six.

Myself, sixteen, with my Uncle Sam
and cousin Siggie
on that fishing trip
to the remote Canadian lakes
where the rivers drain into Hudson's Bay,
Uncle Sam and Siggie
now both deceased.

My sister with her firstborn
on the hill behind our family farm
wearing her father's World War I campaign hat
with a pheasant feather stuck in the band
her son toddling beside her.
He's now forty-six.

Myself with long brown hair,
sideburns, moustache and granny glasses
cradling my infant daughter in one arm.
She's now thirty-nine.

Planned Obsolescence

My hands no longer work the way they used to.
They ache this morning
and I had trouble opening a jar.
Problems too with my wrists, eyes, feet,
shins, shoulders, sacroiliac.
I've had my body in the shop
several times of late
but the wheels still squeak
the steering's loose
and it chugs when going uphill.
Trade-in, however, isn't an option.

The Cookie

Once I was dough
waiting to be shaped.
Then I was baked
and after
I was moist and chewy,
but over time I dried out,
and now I'm beginning to crumble.

Old Men Don't Care What They Wear

They dress for ease and comfort
or with whatever comes readily to hand.
Today I wore tennis shoes
to a restaurant named Demarchelier.
The headwaiter looked down his nose
at which point he might have spied dark sox
if I hadn't happened to have opened the
    drawer
with white ones.
I'd wear ties that are too wide or narrow
if I bothered to wear ties,
my suits were fashionable a generation back
and the style of my eyeglasses
is almost as out of date.
I often stay in my pajamas all day.
I may wear a T-shirt to the pearly gates
and hope St. Peter isn't persnickety
but if he is
I know a less uptight place.

Still Delighting in Snow

I still delight in snow
seventy-some years after I first did.
Though my body now is tentative,
my spirit weary of life's contests,
I still take pleasure
in that world of whiteness
just as I did when I resided
in a frame so small
I can no longer remember how it felt.
Was I an infant?
No way of knowing,
but when I see snow fall
I sense boy-feelings
of those many decades ago,
flakes on my lashes,
the bracing scent,
the compact blizzard
as I tumbled from my sled
a scattering of cold powder
turning my eyebrows white,
as now do other causes,
my clothes encrusted
the wetness soaking through,
the warm kitchen
where I disrobed
("Get out of those wet clothes!"
my mother said)
fading
into the one where I sit now
tapping out this poem.

Still Delighting in Spring

Eighty times
I've witnessed the coming of spring
crocuses, daffodils, jonquils,
hyacinth, narcissus
poking miraculously
out of bare ground,
leaf buds emerging
even more miraculously
from twigs,
stippling woods and neighborhoods
with their fair green,
pointillist pigment of forsythia
dappling yards,
all the signs
that there's life
in the winter-barren matrix
of earth and wood,
and in this old body of mine.

Hyperlinks

My mind is populated with places I've been to,
so many and so diverse.
Driving down a street
in a New Jersey town
an image will flash in my mind
of a street in N'Djamena, Jakarta, Port au Prince
    or Buenos Aires,
or driving through the nearby countryside
I'll suddenly see
an Andean or Punjabi landscape
or one in the Sahel.
A planetful of places, it seems,
is stored inside my skull.

The Inner Child

I know I'm a different person than I was
in my youth
but sometimes it doesn't feel that way.
It's as if all my mistakes had happened
     yesterday
and could happen again tomorrow,
as if I were like a tree
growing by adding layers
with all previous versions nested inside.
Am I unusual in this?
I doubt it.
We think our faults unique
when actually they're common as grass.
There's been much talk in recent years
of the inner child
as if this were a part of us
that's still spontaneous and pure,
when in fact it is, like the original,
full of insecurities and needs
and clamoring for gratification.

Cosmic Questions

Arcturus, Canopus, Alpha Centauri.
When I was a boy
looking up at the night sky
and an older cousin
gave me those names
I was glad to have them
and wondered
what it was like for the men,
bearded and strangely garbed,
who first named those stars
and spun theories about them,
and if beings like us
circled them
and gave them names and stories,
and whether the universe ended
and if it ended
what was outside of it
and how that could end,
or go on forever.
Seventy some years on
I still have few answers
and these are the least of things
of which I'm ignorant.

The Meaning of Life

I've been swimming laps
for almost 70 years
enough perhaps
to circumnavigate the globe,
arms like pistons
legs like paddle wheels,
going nowhere really,
just churning.
Is that what it's all about?

Time Travel

Listening to music from the late 20s
and looking at pictures of Manhattan from that
     time
I imagine my mother and father then,
not long before they met,
she in her late teens,
he in his early 20s.
Imagine isn't a strong enough word.
It's almost as if
I were inhabiting their minds,
my father beginning his working life
with high hopes and ambitions,
my mother barely out of school,
thinking, perhaps, of marriage,
or maybe just her next entertainment,
for that was the jazz era,
flapper times.
And I wasn't even in their minds.

Now, close to a century later,
I can look back
and see what for them was the future,
the Depression,
marriage, divorce and remarriage,
my brothers and sisters,
their children, and mine,
the war, the wars,
buildings rising and falling,
swing, rock n' roll, rap,
computers, smart phones,
a world my parents never could have imagined

but is here before my eyes
as if I'd traveled to another time.

Portrait of My Father

I have a photo of my father
when he was five or six.
We're talking 1908 or 9.
He's standing beside the lake in Michigan
where three generations of our family
spent their summers.
He's barefoot
with dirt on his face
and clothes that are the worse for wear.
He looks like a character from
Tom Sawyer or Huckleberry Finn,
or a painting by Winslow Homer,
but I can recognize in that boy
the man I knew.
I have another photo of him,
one of those formal family portraits,
like a bas-relief at a war memorial,
twenty some people,
my grandparents and their children
and the children's spouses and offspring,
those who were born at that point.
My Dad is in his late 20s,
not long before I was born,
looking pretty much as he would
until he grew old.
But I have no photo of him from the years
    between
and I took to wondering the other day
what he looked like as a schoolboy and teen.
Could you see the man he'd become
in those inchoate features?

The picture is blurry,
like a portrait by Francis Bacon.

Dad

When I was small
and we'd leave some relative's house
where we'd been visiting at night,
my father would carry me to the car
telling me about the stars
and I would ask
"What was there before the stars?"
Or he'd sing to me, and I'd say,
"Daddy, you sing like Bing Crosby."

But that was before I was embarrassed
by his boasting about how much he paid for
    things,
telling visitors
how much the Persian rug in our living room
    cost,
or his Sulka shirts and ties,
and before he began to tell me
"You don't appreciate
how important money is."

We were separated forever
by that tectonic drift,
for he died
before I was capable of seeing his needs
through the glare of my disapproval.

More than a Name

I called my stepfather Dad
but never thought of him as my father.
Once I referred to him as Dad in front of my
    own
and my father was upset.
He needn't have been.
He was the only one in my mind.
Not that he was more affectionate.
But he seemed to have a stake in me
that my stepfather didn't.
He took my successes and failures personally
as if they were his own.
That caused a lot of strain between us
yet it made him my father
in a way my stepfather,
with his lighter touch,
could never have been.

Granny

My grandmother
was ignorant, superstitious, opinionated
and full of odium.
Half old world, half new
she believed nuns were bad luck
like black cats
and was fond of describing people's clothing
as looking like it came out of a cow's behind.

She didn't like girl children
and was hard on her daughter and
    granddaughter
but indulgent toward my brother and me,
pushing food at us
without asking my mother or sister
if they wanted more,
making special dishes for us,
and remarkably tolerant
of our shortcomings,
though she did turn dour
after she found a photograph of a nude
in my dresser, under the socks,
when I was 13.
She didn't say anything about it,
but it disappeared,
and she gave me grim looks
every time our paths crossed
for the next few days.

She was five feet tall
and called herself "peanut granny",

for she had a sense of humor
along with her paranoia and scorn.

She was married twice, and,
not surprisingly,
twice divorced,
and didn't have much education,
but she made her way in business
and took care of herself
without anybody's help,
even giving my mother
a nice sum of money toward a house.

Then she suffered a stroke.
When I visited her in the nursing home
she still recognized me
but called my baby daughter Helen,
which was my mother's name.

Grampa Bill

My mother's father was one of nature's
    gentlemen.
If you'd met him or seen a photo
you'd have thought banker perhaps,
but his career was tending bar.
The earliest picture I have of him
is at the '33 World's Fair
celebrating Chicago's "Century of Progress",
fresh out of Prohibition,
standing with me on his shoulders
in front of the tavern
where he worked.
Earlier he worked in speakeasies
and one of my last memories of him
is behind a bar in the Bowery
presiding over the premises
in his dignified, still easy-speaking way.
I don't know that he ever did any other kind of
    work
except for a short stint in a liquor store
when his health was failing.
I remember my parents
talking *sotto voce*
about what to do for Bill.
My last memory of him is in an oxygen tent
coughing with dignity.

Remembering My Grandfather, Imperfectly

I remember best his grizzled head
and the gnarled hands
he soaked in hot wax.
I remember his legs being bowed
but maybe I imagine that.
And I remember him being not very tall.
Raised in the old country,
the accent of which he still bore,
he probably was shorter than his American
    offspring,
though age had undoubtedly shortened him
    more.
I remember the story of his driving his Model A
through the back of the garage
(which had been a barn)
shouting WHOA as he crashed into the yard.
I only heard about that
though I do remember him often shouting
    "Gud demm!"
But most of all I remember him old.
To me he was always old
for I only knew him when he was,
and I was too wrapped up in my youthful
    preoccupations
to ask him what it was like
when he was young.

The House at the Lake

My grandfather had a house on a lake in
   Michigan
over a hundred miles from Chicago where he
   lived.
I wonder how he found the place
and why it attracted him
an immigrant from Lithuania.
Did it remind him of the lakes of his homeland
or did it just seem a nice place
to get away from the heat of the city?
And why should it seem odd to me
that he took to a lake in Michigan?
Perhaps because he would have seemed so
   alien there
where foreign accents were so rare.

But he was enterprising.
After coming to America
instead of staying in New York
he went west in this to him exotic land
to Chicago where he became a scrap dealer
successful enough to buy a large house
and several acres
on a lake in Michigan,
this little old man
with his thick accent and old-world ways
whom I thought of as a kind of accidental
   appendage
to my American dream.

The Czar's Army

I read an article this morning
by a man whose grandfather fled Russia
to avoid conscription into the Czar's army.
My grandfather did too
and I wonder how many others.
His grandfather ended up in Brooklyn
working the docks,
mine in Chicago
selling scrap.
Others worked as sales clerks
and tailors
and peddlers
beavering away in the new world
so their grandchildren could be
doctors and lawyers and journalists and artists
and write poems about them.
We have the Czar to thank for that.

Born in the U.S.A.

We weren't interested
when we were young
in our grandparents,
with their accents
and musty odors,
nor in the obscure places they came from.
We were part of the new world
and had no need for ancestors
or the lore of old lands.
Now we wish we knew more about them,
but all those who did know are gone.

Uncle Sam

My Uncle Sam,
Shmuel on the other side of the ocean,
my grandmother's brother,
was an odd sort of Yankee Doodle,
(though actually somewhat of a dandy,
in a democratic way)
whose parents, my great-grandparents,
found their way from eastern Europe
to the heartland of America.

He was born in Chicago,
came of age during Prohibition
and worked for bootleggers,
in restaurants, to be sure,
but, nonetheless, on the wrong side of the law,
though he wasn't exactly the criminal type.
He lacked the hard eyes,
and hard insides,
and, while without much schooling,
prided himself on his knowledge of
literature and music,
and produced gorgeous calligraphy,
the kind that graces university degrees,
which might seem to sort oddly
with being employed by gangsters,
but maybe it made them feel
they weren't so far removed
from "the finer things".

I wish I'd had the curiosity
before he passed away
to find out about his dealings, if any,

with the fabled outlaws of the era,
and how he came by his marvelous
   penmanship,
and what his parents were like,
and how things seemed to him as a young man,
but Uncle Sam belonged to those passé
   generations
that were of no interest to me.
This post-Prohibition liquor dealer
with his cultural pretensions
and faint odor of the old world
couldn't compete
with T. S. Eliot.

My Sister Then and Now

In an old photo I have
you're holding a doll
and wearing a ribbon in your hair
too young to imagine
what life may bring.
My arm is around your shoulder.
Our faces are full and smooth
and free of care.

Now you have grandchildren
and suffer infirmities of age.
Yet there's a place in my mind
where you're still that small girl
holding a doll
and wearing a ribbon in your hair.

Silent Treatment

There's an 8x10 photo in my study,
of my sister and me.
It was taken three quarters of a century ago.
I'm nine or ten in the photo
and Nan is two or three.
I'm wearing a tweed suit, and tie,
and Nan a lacey white dress
with frills at the shoulders.
My arm is around her shoulders,
fingers peeping through the frills.
and we're smiling tenderly.

It's three years now
that Nan hasn't talked to me.

Sweet Sue

My cousin Sue was a beauty.
With cascades of curly black hair
set off by a milky complexion,
she looked like the homecoming queen she
    was.
She had a high school sweetheart
whom she later married
but she always turned down other requests for
    dates
with a gentleness that proved exception
to the dictum of a friend of mine,
"Beautiful people are seldom sensitive to the
    needs of others."

They married during the war,
he in his airman's uniform,
and I was there
getting inebriated for the first time in my young
    life.
After two children
he left her for another woman.
Sue went into mourning,
took no interest in other men for years.
She's in her 70s now
but retains
that girlish laughter I remember,
and, I've discovered, an intelligence
I was too intellectual to notice
in my youth.

Family Album

I received some old photos
in the mail today
a gift from another time
from a cousin I spent summers with
over fifty years ago,
and as I studied the pictures
shifting each to the bottom of the stack
a montage of memories
formed in my mind.

We were a group, The Cousins,
populating countryside, lake,
and photographs,
enjoying and suffering one another
through long summer days and evenings
through fun times, boredom and strife,
though good memories
have supplanted bad
in that love of what is no more.

Several snaps of Bob,
who sent the photos
(not Bobby but Bob—
he, being older, dodged the diminutive),
earnestness leaking out around his smile,
responsible for the younger ones,
serious at heart
though he covered youthful insecurity with
    jokes
looking, with his Nordic, Midwestern face,
like one of those boys
who tinkers with cars

and grows up to be an aviator,
which he did.
There's a photo in the stack,
dated '43 on the back,
of him in Army Air Corps uniform
new pilot wings over pocket flap
his arms around his parents' shoulders
a head taller than both
earnestness now well concealed
behind a shavetail grin.

Then there's a snapshot of four of us,
my cousin Lea
chunky then, later large,
in the picture with still unblemished skin
where more recently I saw
sores of diabetic age,
before her heart stopped
earlier this year
that heart so earnestly bent on winning
our childhood games.
"Love ya Dick"
were among the last words I heard her say,
tough to the end
like the life she married
but with love welling up
over childhood rivalries
and years apart.

Dickie
looking furtive and withdrawn,
with his faded-blond hair
and evasive eyes.

A character, I'm told,
in the town where he now lives
in a trailer
perched above the California coast
seen stopping to talk to a professor
from the local university
about his latest interest, Sanskrit.
Wouldn't go to the movies with us as a boy.
His eyes would dart sideways when we asked.
(His mother, my uncle's previous wife,
said movies were sinful.)
Then there were years of mathematics
and paranoia, and drugs
of which he once told his father
"There were times
when you wouldn't have liked knowing me."
Dickie
still alive
and studying Sanskrit.

Then Billy
with a bored smirk
as if to say
"Let's get this shit over with"
looking like one of those kids
you knew just wanted an excuse
to hit you,
and hit he did
with more damage as he got bigger,
and trouble with the law.
He was in the army for a while
then worked in a shipyard.
He called his sister

not long ago
from Tennessee
where he's living now
footloose as ever
the whole country his boxing ring
and invited her to come visit
with her daughter.
They'd smoke some good stuff he said.

And me
looking more confident than I felt
for at least my first thirty years
(how photographs can fool),
looking sensitive
the embryonic poet
with a touch of American Boy
a blend of Rimbaud and Tom Sawyer.
Well, not quite.
But you get the idea.

Bob

As a youth my cousin Bob
was tall and gangling
laughed readily
cracked his knuckles a lot
and introduced the rest of us to chess.
He looked Scandinavian
which he was by extraction
but he also looked like a model,
cut from the Lindbergh mold,
for a Saturday Evening Post cover by Norman
    Rockwell.
It was easy to imagine him
somewhere in the deep Midwest
grease on forehead
bent over a motor,
or in an open cockpit
amidst high piled clouds.
He was in fact a fighter pilot in World War II.
When he came back
he landed in a corporate job
rolling easily into the Eisenhower years,
which is when we lost contact.
But now that we're retired
we exchange Christmas letters.
Turns out he lives in New Hampshire
and is a libertarian,
but likes my poetry.

My Niece the Cowboy

My niece is a wrangler.
No, really.
She rides the range
on the wide Texas plains
with a rifle slung from her saddle,
gelding and branding cattle,
breaking horses
(you need to think like a horse, she says)
fending off coyotes
and wild boar,
and marauding males.
Her address is Mountain Home
where she lives in an unheated cabin
no neighbor in sight,
under a star-crowded sky
with her dogs to keep her warm
on cold nights
this young woman
from the suburbs
my brother the attorney's daughter
an immigrant scrap dealer's great
    granddaughter
far from the shtetl
a roughrider yet
in this age of the internet
this 21st century.

The Fortuneteller

Looking through old photos
it's as if I can see in pictures of the young
what will become of them.
My grandmother in her antique shop,
the entrepreneur,
and later in a nursing home
where she called my infant daughter
by her daughter's name.
My mother at sixteen
a beauty of sophisticated innocence,
destined to marry three times
and die young.
An uncle, dapper in jazz age Chicago,
then in the age of Aquarius
with stroke bent limbs.
A pre-teen brother,
jaunty and impertinent,
now an addict
in his sixties.
A sister's children, five, three and one,
a lawyer, a banker, a professor.

In those photos of our annual family gatherings,
where the adults evolve slowly
from young to middle aged
and middle aged to old
another nephew grows with time-lapse speed
from boy to young man,
but I don't know yet what the fates
have measured out for him.

Metamorphosis

She was thirteen,
more erect in her bearing
sparer in her movements
graver in speech
careful of her dignity,
but occasionally
when younger girls
surrounded her
she would revert
to childish ways
joining coltishly
in their play.

A Work in Progress

I noticed a lamp in the basement today
that my son left there
after he finished school
and seeing it
I picture him reading in a dark room,
his leg draped over the arm of a chair,
in a cone of light from the lamp.
It was like a stage set
and I might have wondered
what would happen next
if I hadn't already known.

As a youth he's interested in architecture
and in high school enrolls in a drafting class
but then one day after school
he informs us
that architects don't earn enough.
He'll major in finance.

Not long after
we meet at the airport in Paris.
I'm on my way back from Africa
with black suitcase and attaché,
he arriving from the States
in jeans and Doc Martins
wearing a backpack
and hefting a duffel bag.
Both of us groggy and disheveled
from overnight flights
we find an inexpensive hotel in Montmartre
and I show him the sights.

A week later it's London
and mega-music stores
then, for my benefit,
a bookstore in Kensington
near our hotel.
I ask Nathaniel if he wants something to read
and he says yes, something amusing.
"Sardonic" I think
and begin going down the shelves
telling him what I think might interest him.
Starting with the A's I skim quickly over Jane
    Austen—
Monty Python and the Simpsons
are more his kind of thing,
along with rap and reggae,
and baseball cards and rotisserie leagues—
but before I've gotten half way through the
    alphabet,
he chooses *Pride and Prejudice*.

Back in school
Nathaniel writes a piece for the school paper,
not the official one, which he disdains,
(along with much else)
but an alternate
started by one of his friends.
The piece,
"The Pleasures of Bench Warming,"
is ostensibly about comradeship and exercise,
but at another level it's about not needing to
    compete,
and at an even deeper level it says,

competition is uncool.
The ultimate form of competition, not to
    compete.

Not long after, we're arriving at the University,
the car loaded with clothes, shoes, books,
    sports equipment
and the lamp, still in its box.
The street in front of the dorm
is crowded with similarly laden station wagons.
Interminable waits at the elevator.
The hall full of excited new students,
parents striving to seem calm
older students greeting each other
with blasé faces.
Were it not for my presence and Nathaniel's
    apparent youth
you would mistake him for one of the latter.
Finance quickly fades.
It requires a first-year course in economics.

E dolce far niente:
several years later
a studio apartment in Paris
(not far removed from a garret)
Nathaniel declaiming about the foolishness
of chaining yourself to a job,
with overtones of
you can't lose if you refuse to play,
and scorn for those who do.
I acknowledge there's something absurd in the
    idea
that work is next to godliness,

and the spectacle of people trying to climb
that figurative greasy pole.
But is there really *niente* enough to last a
    lifetime?

(Flashback:
myself, decades earlier,
at the international calls section
main Post, Telephone and Telegraph office,
the only place in Paris from which
in those good days
you could make an overseas call
if you didn't own a phone.
It's 3AM,
10PM Chicago time,
by the array of clocks on the wall
showing times around the world.
I'm arguing with <u>my</u> father,
something about business school, and being a
    poet, and money.)

We continue, Nathaniel and I,
now arguing political philosophy.
He damns Marxism and capitalism both
with equal opportunity contempt.
Our voices reverberate for several minutes in
    counterpoint.

A year or two later
a call from Nathaniel.
He's going back to school in Paris
to study modern European history.
In the background I see a university building.

Nathaniel disappearing through a door
into a misty interior.

NOT THE END

The Willow

That tree was still youthful when my mother
    died,
that willow now gnarling with age.
If she'd stood by the kitchen window where I
    now stand
she'd have seen the tree,
much smaller then,
and the pond beyond
with its tendrils of early morning mist.
She gardened here
up the hill
where chickens now roost.
It was a cock's crowing—
something,
city dweller,
I hadn't heard in years—
that woke me to the light from another time,
the ghost of that young tree,
the mist above the pond
and the fog shrouded mountain across the
    valley
on which my mother might have gazed
near the end of her too short life.

www.ingramcontent.com/pod-product-compliance
Lightning Source LLC
LaVergne TN
LVHW051734080426
835511LV00018B/3057